SCARY SHARKS

Camilla de la Bédoyère

QEB Publishing

Created for QEB Publishing by Tall Tree Ltd
www.talltreebooks.co.uk
Editors: Jon Richards and Rob Colson
Designer: Jonathan Vipond

Copyright © QEB Publishing, Inc. 2012

Published in the United States by
QEB Publishing, Inc.
3 Wrigley, Suite A
Irvine, CA 92618

www.qed-publishing.co.uk

A CIP record for this book is available from the
Library of Congress.

ISBN 978 1 60992 305 1

Printed in China

Picture credits
(t=top, b=bottom, l=left, r=right, c=centre)
Alamy 26-27 Stephen Frink Collection, 28b
WaterFrame; **FLPA** 20-21 Norbert Wu/Minden
Pictures, 25t D P Wilson, 21b Reinhard Dirscherl,
16-17 Mike Parry/Minden Pictures, 18-19 Norbert
Wu/Minden Pictures; **Getty** 1 Stuart Westmorland,
5b Mark Conlin, 6-7 Doug Perrine; **Nature Picture
Library** 9t Dan Burton, 14b Alan James, 24-25 Doug
Perrine, 28-29 Jeff Rotman, 7b Doug Perrine, 8-9
Doug Perrine, 21t Alex Hyde, 23t David Fleetham,
2-3 Alex Mustard, 22-23 Alex Mustard; **NHPA** 15t
Charles Hood, 4b, 4-5t Burt Jones and Maurine
Shimlock, 12-13t Charles Hood, 12b and 31b Charles
Hood; **Shutterstock** 2-3, 4-5, 10-11, 12-13, 14-15,
30-31 and 32 EpicStockMedia; **SPL** 15b Gerald and
Buff Corsi, Visuals Unlimited, Inc., 17t Andy Murch/
Visuals Unlimited, Inc., 11b Georgette Douwma,
10t Andy Murch, Visuals Unlimited, Inc., 11t Andy
Murch/Visuals Unlimited, Inc., 18b Geoff Kidd

Words in **bold** are explained in the Glossary on page 30.

HOW SCARY?

Look out for this rating. It will tell you how scary and dangerous each shark is!

1 – a bit scary

2 – pretty scary

3 – scary

4 – QUICK! SWIM AWAY!

5 – AAAARGH! TOO LATE!

CONTENTS

Check out this lemon shark on page 22

SUPER PREDATORS

A giant fish swims through the ocean, and its body casts a dark shadow on the seabed below. With its huge teeth, super speed, and cold, dead eyes, this shark is one of the world's most impressive **predators**.

Most sharks are long and thin, but they come in all shapes and sizes. The largest fish in the world is the mighty whale shark. It is harmless to people because it feeds on tiny animals called **plankton**.

Whale sharks are the giants of the ocean and grow to about 36 feet in length.

Frilled sharks have long, thin bodies and live deep underwater.

KILLER FACT

Sharks have been around for 400 million years, and had few predators—until humans began to hunt them.

All sharks are fish. They eat other animals, such as fish and squid. Sometimes, sharks mistake humans for food and attack them. Most sharks are wary of humans, and try to avoid them. There are some scary ones, however, that are more aggressive.

This blue shark has a pointed nose, or snout, and large eyes so that it can see well in deep water.

BULL SHARK

This broad, strong shark is known for its aggressive nature. Bull sharks are described as "short tempered," which means they are always ready for a fight!

Bull sharks usually live and hunt on their own.

Almost all sharks live in seas and oceans, where the water is salty. Bull sharks are more adaptable. They live in shallow coastal waters, but they also swim up rivers, and have even been found in **freshwater** lakes. Spotting a bull shark can be difficult, because they often swim in cloudy water.

KILLER FACT

Some experts believe that the bull shark is the deadliest shark in the world.

SHARK BITES

Length: Up to 11 feet

Habitat: Coasts, rivers, and bays

Where: Warm tropical waters

Weapons: Very aggressive, rapid acceleration, razor-sharp teeth

Lateral line

Sensitive senses

Bull sharks have poor eyesight. Instead, they rely on a superb sense of smell. Like other sharks, they have a sensitive line that runs along their body, called the lateral line. This detects movement and vibrations in the water.

7

GRAY REEF SHARK

Sometimes divers and snorkelers come face-to-face with one of the world's most threatening sharks—the gray reef shark. These hunters patrol coral reefs in groups.

Most sharks are **solitary** animals and live alone. Gray reef sharks, however, often swim in groups in quiet spots during the day. At night they go their separate ways to hunt. When a gray reef shark is feeling threatened it raises its snout, arches its back, and swims with a swaying motion. This menacing behavior warns enemies to move away—or prepare to be attacked.

Fishy feasts

Gray reef sharks feed on squid, octopus, and small shelled animals such as shrimp and lobsters. They also prey on the colorful fish that live among the reefs, such as these beautiful butterfly fish.

SHARK BITES

Length: Up to 8.6 feet

Habitat: Coral reefs

Where: Indian and Pacific Oceans

Weapons: Lots of friends, great agility, and 13–14 rows of teeth

HOW SCARY?

ON THE MOVE

A pointed nose and a streamlined body help a shark to swim fast.

Moving through water is harder work than moving through air. Most fish have a **streamlined** body shape, which means their body moves through water easily. So fast swimmers usually have a long, slender shape.

Most sharks move quickly through water, and their body is packed with powerful muscles. The world's fastest shark is the shortfin mako. It is thought that this shark may reach speeds of 53 miles per hour—that's about the same speed as a cheetah chasing its **prey.**

Pectoral fins control direction and movements up and down.

The dorsal fin helps the fish to swim in S-shaped curves and stops it from rolling over.

The caudal, or tail, fin helps propel the shark through water.

KiLLER FacT

Sharks have a big, oily liver that helps them to float, but if they stop swimming they sink to the seabed.

Slow-movers

Some sharks prefer life in the slow lane. They live on the seafloor and move by swimming and almost "walking" with their fins. This leopard catshark roams the sandy seabed at night, searching for shellfish and small fish.

HAMMERHEAD SHARK

There are about 400 different types, or **species**, of shark and some of the strangest-looking ones are called hammerheads. Like its relatives—such as the mallethead sharks—the great hammerhead has an extraordinary appearance.

A hammerhead's nostrils are far apart, helping it to sense the direction of different smells.

A hammerhead's head is huge and wide, with eyes positioned right at the very ends. This shape probably helps the predator to move through water and change direction. The position of its eyes helps the shark to focus on its prey more easily, and work out how far away it is.

KiLLER FACT

Hammerheads like to feast on venomous stingrays, and can even eat the venom-filled tails!

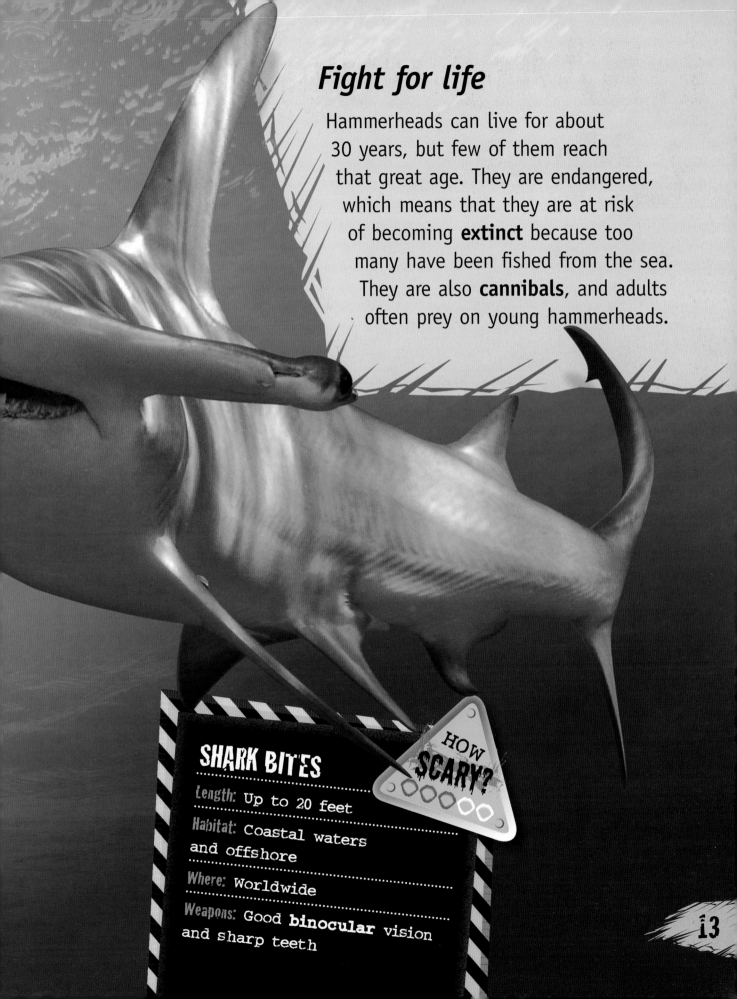

Fight for life

Hammerheads can live for about 30 years, but few of them reach that great age. They are endangered, which means that they are at risk of becoming **extinct** because too many have been fished from the sea. They are also **cannibals**, and adults often prey on young hammerheads.

SHARK BITES

Length: Up to 20 feet

Habitat: Coastal waters and offshore

Where: Worldwide

Weapons: Good **binocular** vision and sharp teeth

HOW
SCARY?

BASKING SHARK

The enormous mouth of a basking shark is large enough to hold a child. Fortunately, a basking shark has no interest in human prey because it only eats tiny plankton!

SHARK BITES

Length: Up to 39 feet

Habitat: Coasts and deep oceans

Where: Worldwide

Weapons: A VERY large mouth and sieve—like plates

HOW **SCARY?**

The largest basking sharks weigh up to 21 tons, five times as much as an elephant.

Water and plankton gush into the shark's huge gaping mouth.

Water passes out through the gill slits but the plankton is caught in the gills.

The huge slits on the side of a basking shark's head are called gill slits. Fish use **gills** instead of lungs to breathe underwater. Water, which contains oxygen, passes into their mouth and out through the gills. Basking sharks also use their gills to feed. Sieve-like plates in the gills trap any plankton in the water.

Actual size!

Plankton

2.4–3.2 in

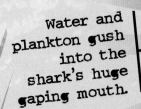

KILLER FACT

Basking sharks often swim near the surface of the sea, and can even leap out of the water!

Mystery shark

Sharks are mysterious creatures, and scientists need to find out much more about their lifestyles. It is known that basking sharks go on long journeys in spring and summer, but no one knows for sure where they disappear to from November to March.

GREAT WHITE SHARK

Does the great white shark really deserve to be called the oceans' most vicious predator? It is certainly well equipped to hunt, catch, and kill its prey.

KILLER FACT

Great whites are amazing swimmers and travel vast distances. In a single year, they have been tracked for over 12,000 miles.

Great whites are special sharks. They are big and powerful, they swim at speed and over great distances, and they are extremely skilled hunters. They can detect a single drop of blood in nearby water.

The good news is that great whites appear to prefer eating fat-filled mammals such as seals and dolphins. They usually reject skinny animals, such as humans, after taking a sample bite.

Great whites have 50 to 60 large teeth that are arranged in rows. When one tooth falls out it is quickly replaced.

Bite and shake

When a great white takes a bite of its prey, it shakes its head from side to side. As it does so, the large triangular teeth saw through the prey, chomping off large pieces of meat.

SHARK BITES

Length: Up to 22 feet

Habitat: Cool coastal waters and deep oceans

Where: Worldwide

Weapons: Powerful muscles, amazing speed, and a crunching bite

HOW SCARY?

TIGER SHARK

Meet the terrifying tiger shark—one of the most dangerous sharks in the world. These predators have been called "bins with fins" because they will try to eat almost anything.

They are called tiger sharks because their skin is marked with dark stripes and spots.

Tiger sharks are hungry, fearless hunters that come close to the shore in search of food. They spend most of the day slowly cruising through the water, but can suddenly burst into speed when they spy something tasty. They hunt sea turtles, clams, stingrays, sea snakes, seals, birds, and squid.

KILLER FACT

Tiger shark teeth are serrated, like a saw. As the sharks bite, they pull their head from side to side and saw the flesh.

HOW SCARY?

Scavengers

These sharks are **scavengers**, which means they are not fussy eaters and will feast on dead meat. They have been found with bottles, lumps of wood, potatoes, car tires—and even drums—in their stomach!

19

SKELETONS AND SCALES

Most fish are bony fish. They have a bony skeleton that gives their body shape, power, and strength. Sharks, however, don't have bones. Instead, their skeleton is made from a strong, bendy material called **cartilage**.

KILLER FACT

It isn't just shark teeth that can hurt—their skin can too. Its rough surface can tear the skin from a swimmer's leg.

Shark denticles

This swell shark has a spotted pattern to help it hide against the seabed.

Shark skin is covered with scales that are coated with enamel—the same tough material that makes our teeth hard. These scales are called **denticles**. Denticles help water to move smoothly over a shark, so it can swim fast.

Colors and patterns

Some sharks have interesting patterns. Colors and patterns can help a shark to stay hidden from view. This is called **camouflage**. This wobbegong shark's strange shape and frilled mouth make a good disguise.

21

LEMON SHARK

Lemon sharks are large coastal sharks. They prefer to live in warm, shallow waters near land, especially during the day. At night they swim to deeper water.

Lemon sharks have a wide, flat head

SHARK BITES

HOW SCARY?

Length: Up to 11 feet

Habitat: Reefs, mangroves, bays, and river mouths

Where: Warm American waters and West Africa

Weapons: Special electrical sensors and triangular teeth

Lemon sharks have small eyes and poor eyesight. The coastal waters where they live are often cloudy, so eyesight is not a great help in finding prey. Instead, these fish have special magnetic **sensors** in their snout, which help them to find fish and shelled animals on the seabed.

Sharksuckers

Remoras, or sharksuckers, are long, thin fish with a special ability. They have a sucker on the top of their head, which they use to stick to a shark or other large fish and hitch a ride. They feed off any scraps that the shark does not eat.

Lemon sharks get their name from the yellow–brown color of their skin.

23

EGGS AND PUPS

Most fish lay eggs that hatch into baby fish. Sharks are special, though. Many of them don't lay eggs, they give birth to their young instead. Young sharks are called **pups**.

Lemon sharks can give birth to as many as 17 pups in a single year.

Most mother sharks keep their pups inside their body while they grow. This means the pups are protected from predators for as long as possible. When the pups are born they are able to swim away. Sharks don't look after their pups.

Mermaid's purse

Sharks that do lay eggs, such as catsharks, lay the eggs in a thick, rubbery case called a mermaid's purse. These egg cases often have curly strings, which attach them to rocks or seaweed to stop them from floating away. The shark pups grow inside for up to ten months.

2.4–3.2 inches

Actual size!

This newborn lemon shark pup swims away from its mother.

KILLER FACT

Pups growing inside their mother may eat each other before they are even born. Sometimes only one or two pups survive.

LONGNOSE SAWSHARK

This small shark has a peculiar snout that makes up more than one quarter of its whole body length. The shark uses its strange nose, called a rostrum, as a lethal weapon and to detect prey.

The sides of the long nose are lined with rows of teeth.

up to 17.6 inches

Sawsharks have a small, flat body because they live on the seabed and swim close to the bottom, where they hunt for small fish, squid, and shrimp. Their long nose is called a saw and is lined with long, sharp teeth. Long feelers on the saw, called barbels, are used for touch. They also have teeth in their jaws, which they use for biting.

As they cruise along the seabed, sawsharks use their barbels to detect prey hidden in the sand and mud.

SHARK BITES

Length: Up to 4.6 feet

Habitat: Seabed in coastal areas

Where: Southern Australia

Weapons: Sensitive detectors and small, needle-sharp teeth

KILLER FACT

Sawsharks sense electricity using organs called ampullae of Lorenzini. These are small, gel-filled holes in their saw.

Electric sense

These sharks use their saw to swipe at their prey, or to rake through mud and dislodge animals hiding there. Their saw has another great use too—it can detect electricity. All animals use electricity to make their muscles work, and sharks have a super-sense that helps them to detect it.

27

SHARKS AND PEOPLE

Humans are much more deadly than sharks. It is rare for sharks to attack people, and most of those human victims do survive an attack. People, however, kill up to 120 million sharks every year.

Many of these majestic marine predators are now in grave danger of becoming extinct. That means they will disappear from our planet forever. Sharks are fished from the seas for their meat and their fins, which are used in soup. They are also caught accidentally by fishermen who are hoping to catch other fish to eat.

This dogfish died after getting tangled in a fisherman's net.

Shark cages allow
scientists to study
sharks close—up,
without either
the divers or the
sharks getting
into trouble.

Saving sharks

We need sharks in our seas. They are
part of the ocean ecosystem, and they
play an important part in keeping the
oceans healthy and in balance. We can
help by not buying shark products, and
by learning as much as we can about

KILLER FACT

There used to be ten
times as many sharks
in the oceans as there
are today.

GLOSSARY

binocular
Seeing using both eyes together. Binocular vision is good for hunting.

cannibals
Animals that eat others from the same species.

cartilage
A strong, flexible fiber in animals' bodies. Sharks' skeletons are made from cartilage.

camouflage
A pattern of colors on an animal's body that hides it from predators or prey.

denticles
Hard scales on a shark's skin that help it to swim faster.

extinct
A species of animal that is no longer alive.

freshwater
Water without salt in it, such as that found in lakes and rivers.

gills
Organs used by fish to breathe. The gills collect oxygen that is dissolved in the water.

plankton
Small animals and plants that float in the oceans, carried along by the ocean currents.

predators
Animals that hunt other animals to eat.

prey
Animals that are hunted by predators.

pup
The young of a shark.

scavenger
An animal that feeds on dead animals or plants that it finds. Some sharks are scavengers.

sensors
Organs in an animal that respond to stimuli such as light or magnetism.

solitary
Living alone, away from other members of the same species.

species
A kind of animal or plant. Members of the same species are able to breed, producing young.

streamlined
A smooth shape that allows fluids such as water to flow easily around it.

TAKING IT FARTHER

What makes a shark "scary"? Now it's time for you to decide.

- Choose some scary features, such as speed, size, habitat, aggressive personality, and favorite food.

- Use this book, and the internet, to award up to five points for each of a shark's scary features. Repeat for as many sharks as you want.

- Turn your results into a table, graph, or chart. Add up the totals to get a "Scary Score" for each type of shark.

USEFUL WEBSITES

www.sharktrust.org
Discover more about the interesting world of sharks.

www.flmnh.ufl. edu/fish/sharks
A great website for finding up-to-date information on sharks.

ocean.nationalgeographic. com/ocean
For facts and photos about sharks and their habitat.

www.arkive.org
Essential information on

TOP 5 DEADLY SHARK FACTS!

- Sharks can see in dark water, but they are probably color-blind.

- One big meal is enough to keep some sharks alive for many months.

- Sharks lose thousands of teeth over a lifetime, but new ones replace them.

- There are nearly 400 different types of shark, but only about 12 of them are dangerous to humans.

- The smallest shark in the world, the dwarf lanternshark, grows to just 7.9 inches long.

INDEX